As you read the book, you can print off any linked worksheets from www.llttf.com/resources to allow you to practice the skills you are learning (free registration).

Download from

www.llttf.com/resources

Look out for this image to highlight these free resources.

You feel bad because you're in a vicious cycle

The way you feel is often affected by things that happen to you. Like the things on the opposite page. The different situations are all outside you. Sometimes, you can change what's happening outside, but often you can't do much about them.

And when you allow them to affect your mood, the vicious cycle kicks in and you feel worse and worse and worse…

Vicious cycles spin by affecting five areas™ of your life.

Turn over to see how it works

Example: Forgot your friend's birthday

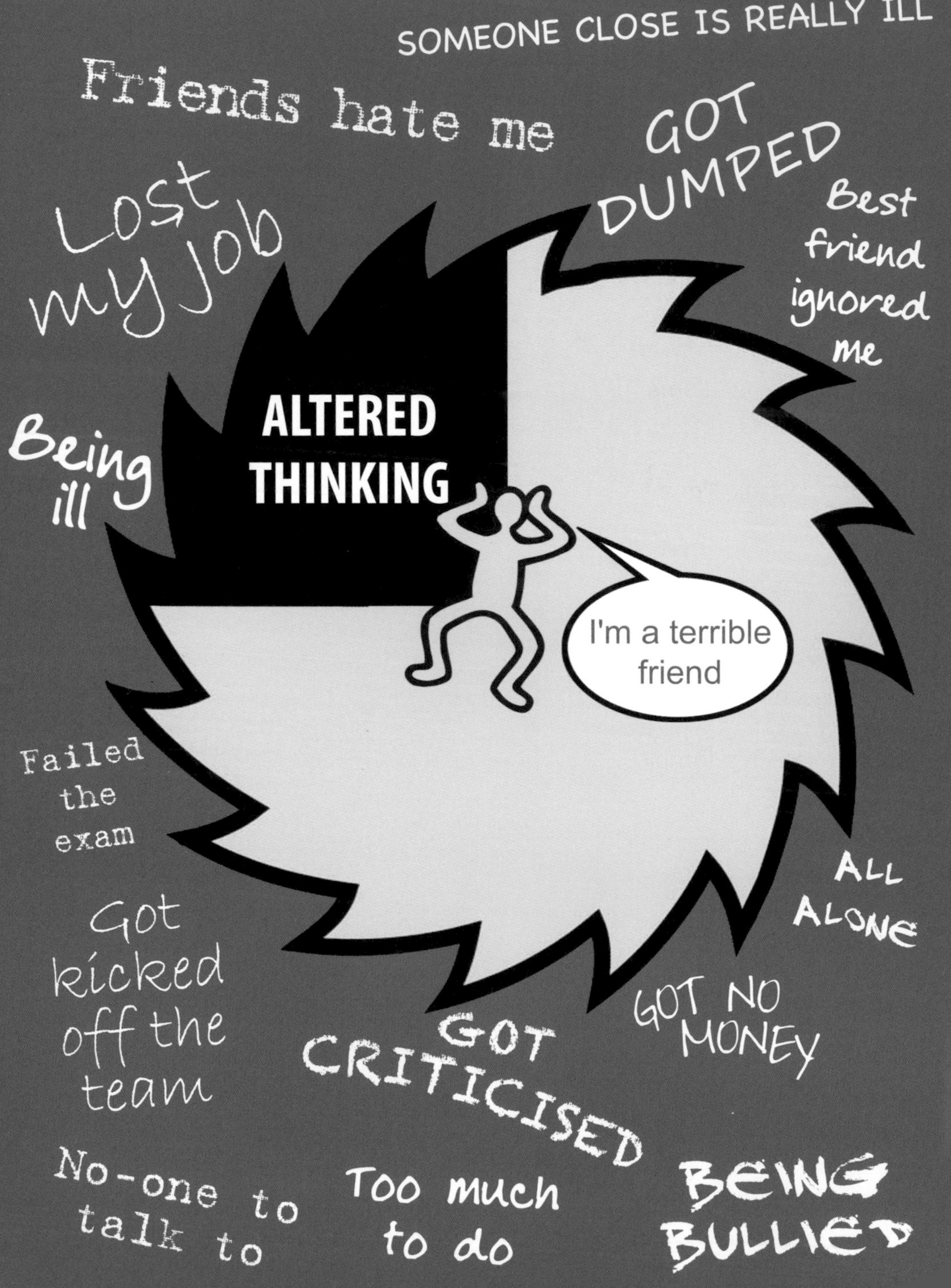

First...
1. An outside event affects you

When something happens, you naturally notice it and think about it. If you forget your friend's birthday, for example, you may think "I'm a terrible friend!". This is called **Altered Thinking.**

Altered thinking can set off a chain reaction inside you that affects the way you feel and what you do.

When your altered thinking is unhelpful (like "I'm a terrible friend"), the vicious cycle is triggered and you can end up really down, not getting out of bed and even feeling sick.

Let's see the Vicious Cycle in action

Example: Forgot your friend's birthday

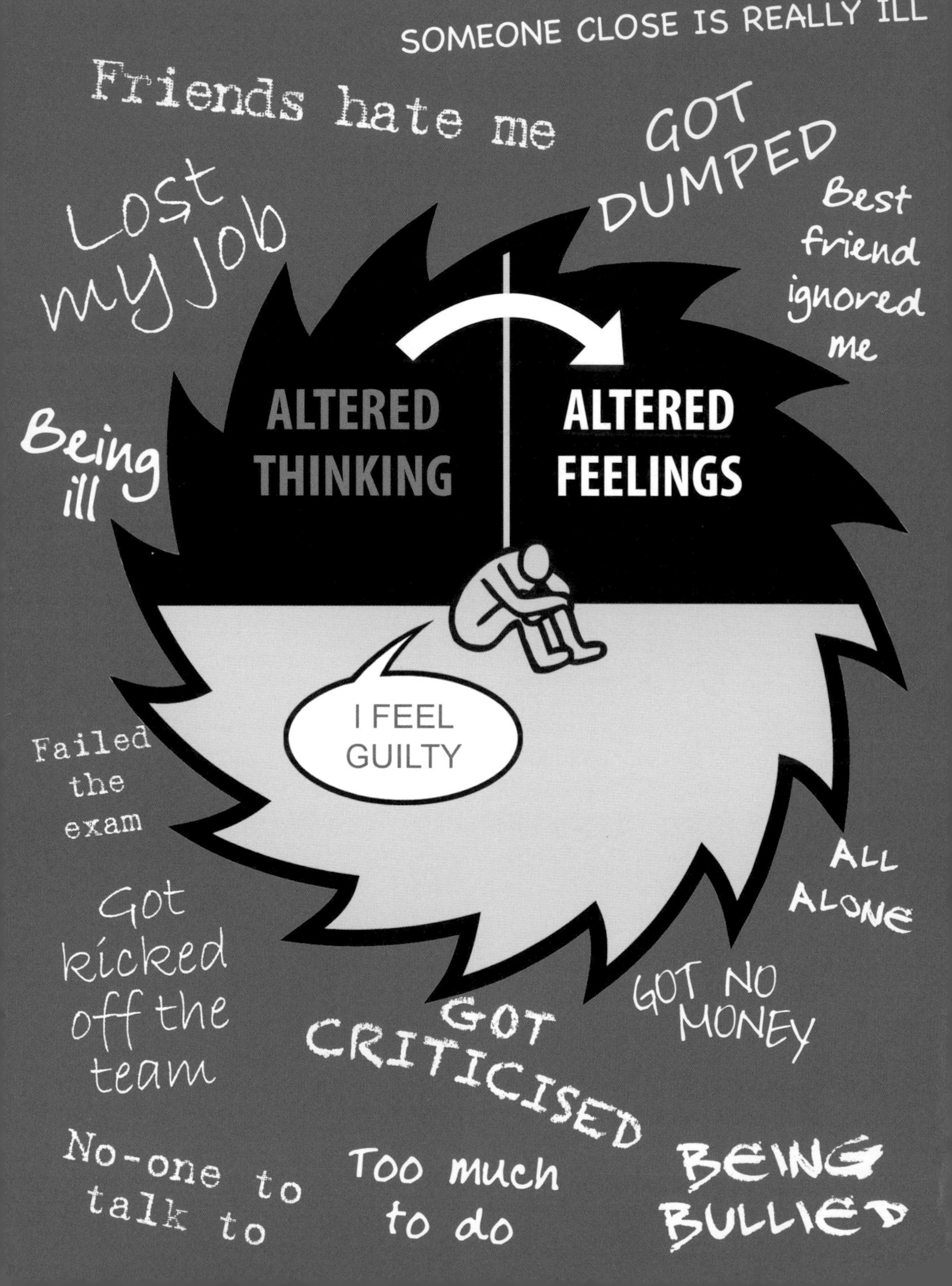

2. Altered thinking leads to...
3. Altered feelings

If you think "I'm a terrible friend!" you're likely to feel pretty low, sad or guilty.

Maybe you think that you've let your friend down, or you might feel guilty because you know you should have been more organised.

So now what happens?

Example: Forgot your friend's birthday

SOMEONE CLOSE IS REALLY ILL

Friends hate me

GOT DUMPED

Best friend ignored me

LOST my JOB

Being ill

ALTERED THINKING

ALTERED FEELINGS

I'VE GOT TUMMY ACHE

ALTERED PHYSICAL SENSATIONS

Failed the exam

ALL ALONE

Got kicked off the team

GOT CRITICISED

GOT NO MONEY

No-one to talk to

Too much to do

BEING BULLIED

Altered feelings lead to...
4. Altered physical sensations

When you feel low or guilty, you can get sweaty and tense and your stomach or your head can ache. Sometimes you can feel really tired.

Your hands might feel clammy, or you feel really tense and can't sit still.

Ever had a sinking feeling or felt your heart racing? It's probably that old vicious cycle spinning round!

What next?

Example: Forgot your friend's birthday

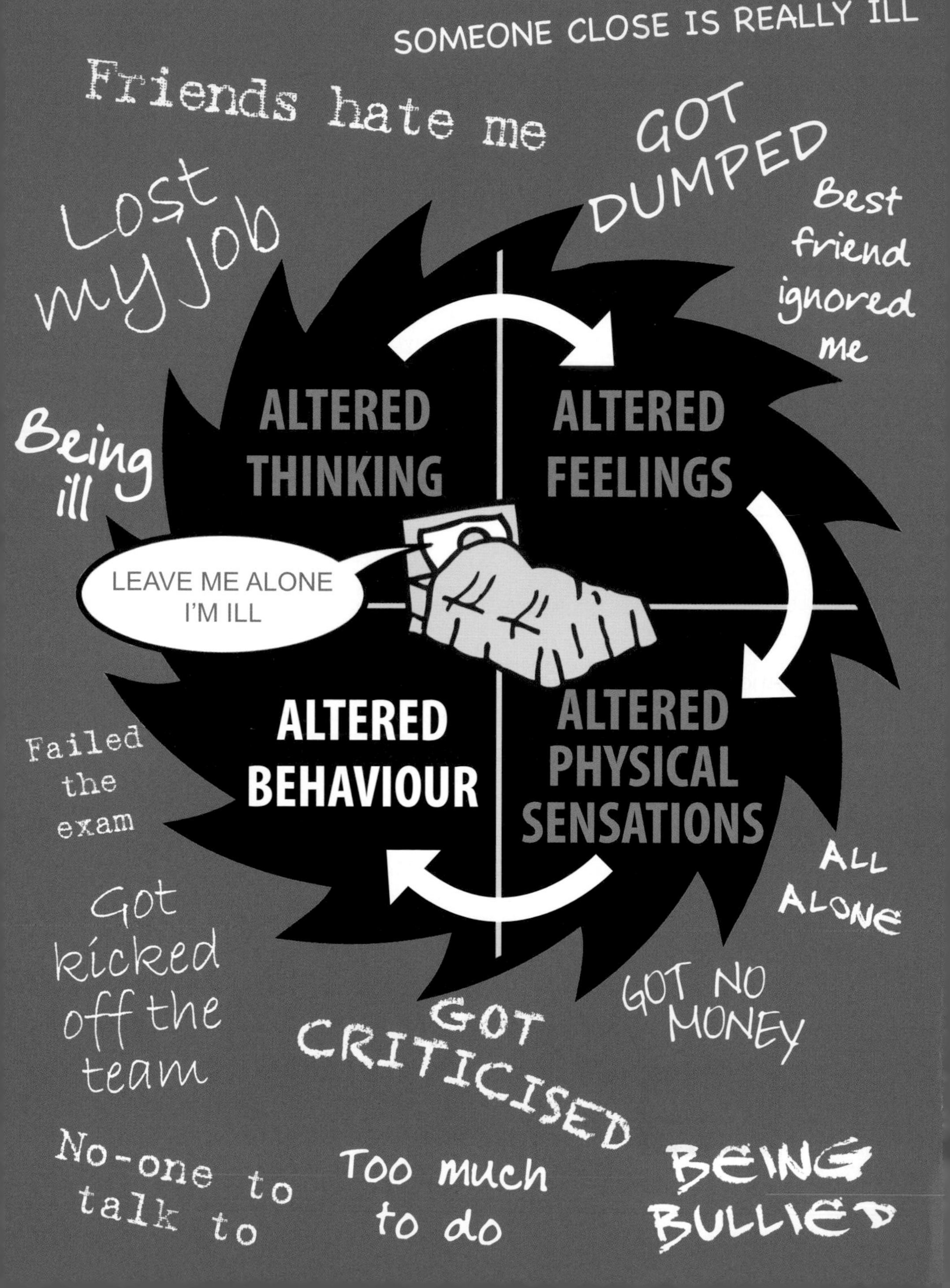

Altered physical sensations lead to...
5. Altered behaviour

It's only natural. You're really tired, you have a headache or maybe feel tense, so you don't feel like going out, or even getting up. You steer clear of people who might ask if you sent a card or present. You start to feel worse, and the worse you feel, the less you do. You stay in and hardly do any exercise. You're not eating right and you seem to catch all the bugs that are going round.

You even finish up at the doctor's, asking why you can't seem to shake off this virus you've had for weeks.

And you know what happens then? The cycle goes round again, only this time, you're avoiding people, staying in bed and fed up, so you get even worse.

Vicious, these cycles, aren't they? That's why it's important to work out how these five areas™ of life (outside events, thinking, feelings, physical symptoms and behaviour) are changing how you feel.

Now what about you?

11

COMPLETE YOUR OWN FIVE AREAS™ ASSESSMENT

You've read about how you might react if you missed your friend's birthday. Do you fall into other vicious cycles from time to time?

Here's how to play detective and work out how the vicious cycle affects you.

Choose a recent time when you felt worse emotionally or physically. To start with, don't pick a time that is really upsetting or distressing. Instead choose a situation when you felt a bit down, fed up, angry, stressed, scared, frustrated, guilty, ashamed, tired, or in pain.

Now use the next two pages to work out how you reacted.

Pen at the ready?

Now's time to spot that vicious cycle!

MY
FIVE AREAS™
ASSESSMENT

Understanding Feelings

What's going on? Describe the situation:

My thoughts. Am I:
- ☐ Beating myself up?
- ☐ Focusing on the bad stuff?
- ☐ Being gloomy about the future?
- ☐ Expecting things to go wrong?
- ☐ Worrying what others may think about me?
- ☐ Other _____

My feelings. Do I feel:
- ☐ Low/Sad?
- ☐ Stressed/Anxious?
- ☐ Guilty?
- ☐ Ashamed?
- ☐ Angry/Irritable?
- ☐ Other

_____

Altered Thinking

Altered Feelings

Altered Behaviour

Altered Physical Sensations

My behaviour. Am I choosing to:
- ☐ Avoid something?
- ☐ Escape/Run away?
- ☐ Lean on others too much?
- ☐ Stop doing fun things?
- ☐ Stop seeing people I like?
- ☐ Doing things that can backfire?
- ☐ Other _____

- ☐ Shaky?
- ☐ Can't sleep?
- ☐ Heart racing?
- ☐ Dizzy?
- ☐ Other _____

My body. Am I:
- ☐ Tense?
- ☐ Sick?
- ☐ Off my food?
- ☐ Hot/Sweaty?
- ☐ Tired out?
- ☐ Cold/Clammy?
- ☐ Not able to relax?

YOUR
VICIOUS
CYCLE

Did you fall into a vicious cycle?

If you felt bad, it's likely the vicious cycle was spinning. Was there an outside event - like a person or difficult situation - or something that was said of went wrong? Did what you think affect how you felt – in your feelings and physical symptoms? How did this affect what you did?

Did anything look familiar? Patterns of thinking, feeling or body reactions often repeat like habits again and again. Did the cycle start to spin and make you feel even worse?

Stopping your cycle spinning takes practise. If you're feeling worse than usual it can feel hard to break the cycle.

Now for the *good* news!

YOU
CAN
STOP
THE CYCLE!

You know the great thing about cycles?
They turn both ways!

In the same way that just one thing (often
an altered thought) led to everything else
getting worse, you can start to make it
better by changing one thing.

Just by acting differently, or changing the
way you think about things, you can
change **all the other things in the cycle**
and start to feel better. You can change the
vicious cycle into a **virtuous cycle.**

Sounds too easy? Turn over for an
example.

How to stop the cycle

Example: The Cycle in action

1 **Situation:** You're walking down the street and someone you know walks by and doesn't say hello or smile.

2 **Altered thinking.** You jump to the conclusion they don't like you.

Oh no! She doesn't like me!

3 **Altered feelings.** This makes you feel bad.

Oh no! She doesn't like me!

I feel down

4

Altered physical sensations.
You have no energy and maybe can't sleep that night for worrying about what happened.

Oh no! She doesn't like me! | I feel down | I feel tired and exhausted

5

Altered behaviour.
You go home and avoid other people's company.

Oh no! She doesn't like me! | I feel down | I stop seeing people | I feel tired and exhausted

and the Cycle spins....

21

Example: How to break the Vicious Cycle and create a Virtuous Cycle

1 **Situation:** You're walking down the street and someone you know walks by and doesn't say hello or smile.

2 **Altered thinking.** You look at things differently.

Poor Louise, she must be upset, I wonder what's wrong?

3 **Altered feelings.** You feel concerned and worried for Louise.

Poor Louise, she must be upset.

Feel concerned for Louise

4 **Altered physical sensations.** You feel energised to help.

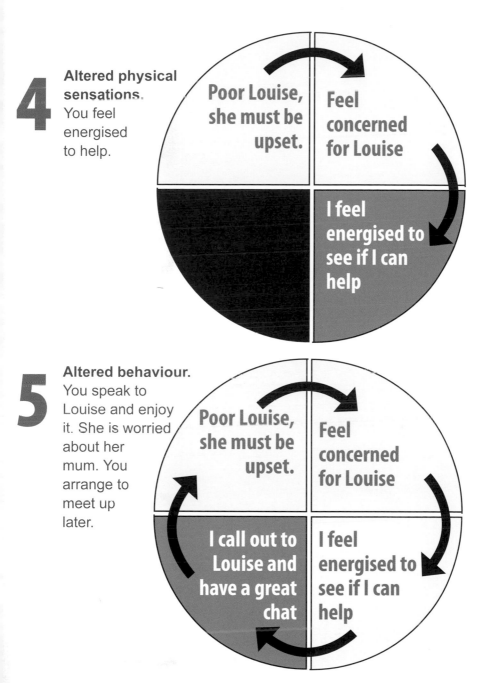

Poor Louise, she must be upset.

Feel concerned for Louise

I feel energised to see if I can help

5 **Altered behaviour.** You speak to Louise and enjoy it. She is worried about her mum. You arrange to meet up later.

Poor Louise, she must be upset.

Feel concerned for Louise

I call out to Louise and have a great chat

I feel energised to see if I can help

YOU HAVE THE CHOICE

The cycle can come in any sequence of thoughts/feelings/ bodily sensations and behaviour.

You can break the cycle by changing any of these areas.

You just need to change one thing

You can break the vicious cycle by changing just one thing – your thinking, your response, your activities – almost anything. And it doesn't have to be a big thing!

You could start by changing the way you respond. By going out just one time. By doing just a bit more exercise. By changing the way you think about things. By meeting up with a friend, tackling a problem, or by choosing not to do something that will make things worse.

If you manage to do something about just one thing, you'll break the vicious cycle, stop it spinning down and down and start to feel better straight away.

So here's what to do. Pick one small thing then use the **Planner sheet** on the pages that follow to give yourself the best start.

Once you're done, use the **Review sheet** on the two pages after the Planner to check your progress.

Go, make a plan!

Planner Sheet

Make a Plan!

1. What am I going to do?

Just one small thing

2. When am I going to do it?

That way you'll know if you don't do it

3. What problems or difficulties could arise, and how can I overcome them?

4. Is my planned task -

	Yes	No
• Useful for understanding or changing how I am?	☐	☐
• Specific, so that I will know when I have done it?	☐	☐
• Realistic, practical and achievable?	☐	☐

My notes:

Review Sheet

How did it go? What did you plan to do?

Did you try to do it?   Yes ☐   No ☐

If yes: What went well?

What didn't go so well?

What have you learned from what happened?

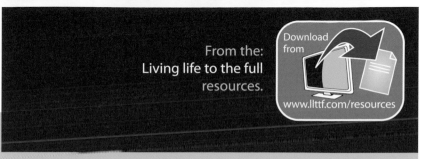
How are you going to apply what you have learned?

If no: What stopped you?

You: (forgot, not enough time, put it off, didn't think I could do it, couldn't see the point etc.)

Other things: (other people, work or home issues, poor weather, transport difficulties etc.)

How can you tackle things differently next time?

Next steps...

Use the five areas™ vicious cycle to make sense of why you feel the way you do. Remember, that's not all you've discovered. You've also learned some things to change that will make a big difference.

What changes do you need to make in each of the five areas? When you've worked on your current problem, you might want to choose another area and work on something else in your life.

You can get added help and support at www.llttf.com - the award-winning web course. It's also the most recommended online resource for anxiety and depression by NHS England.*

Go for it!

*Bennion et al, 2017. BMJ Open http://bmjopen.bmj.com/content/7/1/e014844